# Embedding Safer Workplace free of Sexual Harassment into your Organization's DNA

I0487999

Copyright © 2019 Capt Tapas Majumdar

------------------------------------------------------------------

ISBN #: 978-0-359-75737-4

------------------------------------------------------------------

Content ID: 24888719

------------------------------------------------------------------

Self-published in 2019.

All rights reserved. No part of this publication may be reproduced or distributed in any Form or by any means, or stored in a data base or retrieval system, without the prior Written permission of the author.

This publication is designed to provide useful and authoritative Information for business owners. It is sold under the express understanding that any Decisions or actions you take as a result of reading this book must be based on your Commercial judgement and will be at your sole risk. The author will not be held Responsible for the consequences of any actions.

# Acknowledgements

Sexual harassment at the workplace is a real and current crisis. I would want to thank **Leighton Asia** and our group company **CIMIC group** who gave me the opportunity to understand this challenge that our society faces and lead the India initiative in dealing with it. The group has not just limited itself to defining policies around diversity & inclusion but has and is currently incorporating it as part of our daily life at work. They have always endeavoured to promote diversity and inclusion in letter and spirit; specifically, prevention of sexual harassment. I have had the opportunity to lead many initiatives for the India business and the more I interacted on the subject the more I got involved and convinced on the criticality of this initiative. Subsequently I was encouraged to take structured learning on the subject to have a sound understanding of the legal

# Embedding safer workplace free of sexual harassment into your organization's DNA

Capt Tapas Majumdar

issues and complexities involved across cultures across geographies.

# Preface

The Charter of the United Nations reaffirms faith in fundamental human rights, in the dignity and worth of the human person and in the equal rights of men and women, and that the Universal Declaration of Human Rights affirms the principle of the inadmissibility of discrimination and proclaims that all human beings are born free and equal in dignity and rights and that everyone is entitled to all the rights and freedoms set forth therein, without distinction of any kind, including distinction based on sex. Sexual harassment is a violation of Human Rights of an individual and must be unacceptable to anyone regardless of the cultural background or nationality. It is something that all us, on humanitarian grounds must stand up against and set it right in our own ways possible.

Sexual harassment at the workplace is a global issue and has similar construct and challenges regardless of nationality or cultural background. The laws on prevention of sexual harassment is at different stages of maturity in many countries. However, they are quite similar in nature with variations specific the maturity stages of different countries and societies. The ones that are evolving are taking the leads from those countries who have a well-developed policy and procedures, while staying relevant to their respective cultures.

For the purpose of this book, I have used the laws enacted in India as a base to explain certain important concept. However, the learnings are not restricted to India, readers from across all countries would be able to connect.

My learnings over these few years of being involved, is that Sexual harassment at the workplace is a culture issue and the needs to be addressed from a culture point of view. Legislations can only support and reinforce, at best it can be a deterrence. Deterrence is important but cannot stand up in isolation. The key lies in the influencing the work culture within your workplaces. This is something that you can influence and control. My argument towards making your workplace safer and free of sexual harassment is channelized through the lanes and by lanes of work culture.

# Table of Contents

# About Capt Tapas Majumdar (retd)

Capt Tapas Majumdar is a

practicing Senior HR

Professional with hands on

experience in leading HR

Function and Business

Functions in India and abroad. A Certified Corporate

Director from Institute of Directors, 6 Sigma Green Belt

from ECG USA, Master's Degree Holder in HR and an ex-

army officer, who knows how to drive Employee and

Process Productivity, drive Profitability, Build Successful

Leadership Teams, and Lead Business Functions.

Capt Tapas has led the ethics committees and has

experience in investigating into matters of ethics, code of

conduct, prevention of sexual harassment and modern

slavery. He is a member of Internal Complaint's Committee

and has designed and rolled out POSH policies and Trained Internal Committee Members on conducting investigations.

23 years of experience in leadership roles across 7 industries covering the entire gamut of Human Resource, in addition to Corporate Governance and Diversity & Inclusion at the Strategic Level. His areas of specialization include HR Systems and Process, Strategy Implementation, Gender Diversity & Inclusion and Corporate Governance.

He has served the Indian army as an Infantry Officer and is a visiting faculty with management institutes like NMIMS & IES and technical institutes like CDAC and Guest Speaker with SP Jain. Capt Tapas is a Management graduate with a Master's in Human Resources Development and Management from NMIMS, Mumbai University, India.

# Chapter1: Sexual Harassment at workplace: An important perspective

Sexual harassment is a displayed behavior, it is the act that leads to harassment, but when does the act begin to harass and why many people are unable to understand that their act is causing harassment. Even worse, why do some people choose to ignore the resistance of the victim considering it as an expected behavior and why do some have an air of defiance around them that considers them supreme and that they are entitled. Why do majority of the victims do not stand up openly to harassment. Why the culture of silence, where the victim does not want to report it because of multiple fear of social stigma and bringing disrepute to self and family. Why are such behaviors, often unconscious, be part of 'Normal'? Understanding of this 'behavior' as 'normal' or 'acceptable' in society at large is important to deal with the issues of Sexual harassment at the workplace. Many cases of harassment do not start with the intent to harass, but eventually results in one. Often when there is no consent, many do not know how to handle them. Whether a victim or the aggressor, their lack of maturity or knowledge in not knowing the right way to deal with it often leads to serious irreversible physical, mental and emotional damage and sometimes even fatality. There are many questions that can be asked as we observe cases with a logical mind, but we also know that none of us operate in isolation, we are part of a society, and a society has a culture and cultures have norms, beliefs and traditions. Sexual harassment is a social issue routed in culture the society develops. There is no disputing the fact that the relations between sexual harassment and culture is a complex one. It is the culture that shapes behaviors of individuals, the concept of 'right' or 'wrong' is germinated in the ecosystem of culture.

## Societal culture and work culture

Culture is something that we experience. It has a very broad definition and has been defined differently by many experts. From a point of our understanding, culture can be understood as a set of beliefs, value system, knowledge and norms that is passed on from one generation to the next. It is alive and vibrant. The believes and value systems develop over a period of a long time. People from the culture continuously interact with the outside world and keeps adapting. Whatever that works for them is repeated and if largely successful it is adopted as a practice. Let me take an example here, why do some cultures require women to wear veils? Let us consider the 'parda' system that has existed in India and the 'burka' system that has existed in other cultures as well for a long time. Both systems existed in different parts of our world that were not connected directly since the medieval times. Today many intellectuals find the system oppressive and discriminatory and a symbol of women inequality. Many women feel that it frees them from unwelcomed male advances and objectifying them. Both have its origins in rise of constant conflicts and wars, lawlessness that was their reality. Cultures learnt from the environment that they were in and adapted, the adaptation worked for them and it was included as a tradition or a norm. If today we feel that there should be no need for these systems to exist, is attributed to changes in the environment, women today are better protected by law and are given equal status. These changes in the environment is resulting in our cultures adapting and creating new traditions and norms. The not so good news is that these changes are not immediate, it takes time and not all people living in the culture change all at the same time… it takes time. Same sex marriages and live in relationships are some of the other changes happening in societies.

The adaptation of the culture to its environment is transmitted to the next generations as traditions. It forms a critical part of our culture and structures the foundations of families and social behavior and individual behavior. It facilitates interactions within the members of the culture and has a higher degree of comfort, as it exudes predictable behavior. It is through traditions, that behavior of individual members from a culture are guided and the understanding of 'right' and wrong' emerges. It would be worthwhile to know that traditions are well engrained in a deeper sense, whether scientific or otherwise.

On the other hand, Work culture is structured on similar on the lines of culture within a society. It is made up of such traits shared by a group of people. Culture is the behavior that results when a group arrives at a set of generally unspoken and unwritten rules of engagement or behavior referred to as norms. Work culture can be understood as the culture within the organization. It comprises of sets of values systems, beliefs, knowledge and norms that the organization follows. Work cultures also keeps interacting with its environment and keeps adapting over a period. This keeps the work culture alive and kicking. The of values systems, beliefs, knowledge and norms in the work culture are learned. People learn to perform certain behaviors through either the rewards or negative consequences that follow their behavior, i.e. through negative or positive reinforcements. When a behavior is rewarded, it is repeated, and when it is not accepted or results in a punitive action it is discarded, this eventually becomes part of the work culture.

Work culture is learned through interaction. Employees contribute to the work culture by interacting with other employees internally and with members of the external environment like vendors, clients etc. Most behaviors and rewards in organizations involve other employees. An applicant experiences a sense of your work culture and his or her fit within your work culture during the interview process. An initial opinion of your work culture can be formed as early as the first phone call from the human resources department. The work culture that a new employee experiences and learns can be consciously shaped by managers, executives, and co-workers. Through your conversations with a new employee, you can communicate the elements of the work culture you'd like to see continued. If this interaction doesn't take place, the new employee forms his or her own idea of the work culture, often in interaction with other new employees.

People shape the work culture especially at the top of the management ladder. Personalities and experiences of employees create the culture of an organization. Different employees experience differently and hence may have different understanding of the internal and external changes impacting the culture. These experiences are debated and argues, often passionately that eventually arrives at a negotiated work culture. This increases the ownership of the work culture amongst employees.

## Contextual understanding of Societal Culture and Work Culture

There is a difference between work culture and culture within a society. The difference essentially lies in the genesis of both types of cultures. Let's talk about this a bit, it has an important influence on sexual harassment at workplace and can give a different perspective to organizations in dealing with such cases and even effectively preventing them.

None of us live in isolation, we are part of a culture, a culture that we were born into. Now that was not by choice, unless we have memories of our pre-birth period. The place, time and to whom we are born is not by our choice. Our initial learning phase is on a clean slate. We abide by what our elders tell us and even more from what they do. Learn from what our teachers and others teach us. These are the faith, belief, values, knowledge and norms that are being passed on to us by the previous generation. This has its origins in the culture of the society that we have been born into. This eventually gets framed in our minds and gives us a sense of 'right' and 'wrong'. When our behavior is violative of these, it is the pressure of the other members that makes us toe the line, these are the norms. On the extreme, this could better explain societal incidences like 'honour killing', 'female foeticide', 'role definition of sexes' and 'segregated behavior' towards them. However, in case of work culture, people of different societal cultures come together for a common purpose. This purpose generally relates to having successful careers, providing for self and families. meeting aspirations, earning more money.

One of the major reasons for many people originates from the societal culture norm of being financially independent, to be able to support a family and the need to be a productive and a contributing member of the family, for recognition, image in the society, or even social status. Hence the drive for promotions, designations and money.

People while associated with work cultures have a greater sense of purpose, there is a need that drives behaviors. The drive of security, safety, status, achievement, self-actualization are amongst the predominant drives. While being associated with societal culture, social acceptance, status and self-actualization are more in focus. There is greater acceptability to new learnings while associated with work cultures, the interactions with people from other cultures that may even have contradictory traditions, faiths, beliefs and norms as compared to the societal culture that the person comes from is far more acceptable. Work cultures define the 'acceptable' and 'not acceptable' behaviors. Every new person joining the work culture undergoes an integration process that includes the clash of beliefs and values, often referred to as the storming phase and then the balance is struck, which is the norming phase. In the societal culture, you are born into it, that is your first learning and hence there is no conflict. You interact with people from within the culture who encourage and reinforce compliance to the existing norms.

Thus, it can be understood that the same person can be an effective and contributing member of both the cultures simultaneously.

## Sexual harassment at the workplace and the culture of silence

Sexual harassment at the workplace has existed for a long time. It Is comparatively only recently, that they are being brought to the fore. Some of the incidences have occurred decades ago. While it is easy to sit in judgement today and question as to why they were not brought to the fore then, it is important to remember that the prevalent culture and the norms were different. The fact that we are more openly voicing ourselves and standing up to such incidences in large numbers, and why were we not able to do so earlier. The response is pretty much the same, the good news is that societal culture and it's norms, traditions, value systems and knowledge is being upgraded continuously. The culture of silence is majorly driven by power. The victim feels that the aggressor has the capability to exert his "Power", whether, physical, emotional or any other that will bring more harm and that the cost of silence is far lesser than the cost of disclosure. The feel of power by the victim may be real or may be perceived, the resultant action is the same. There is a heightened sense of 'consequence' and 'helplessness', again it is either real or perceived. There are other reasons to this as well. This pertains to early childhood grooming of the victim. If the victim has a low self-worth, the chances are that silence will prevail. The feeling of being dispensable and generally not taken seriously, impacts the victim's reaction towards sexual harassment. Early childhood grooming does play a major role in the course of action that follows. A culture of silence only emboldens the aggressor and sends out wrong message of 'acceptable' behavior at the workplace.

Others who witness such incidence are also part of this culture of silence. Given that they are not directly affected the instinctive decision whether to 'get involved' or no is based on multiple factors, prime amongst them is their 'instinct of self-preservation'. This is an unlearned behavior that makes the witness do a quick assessment if there is any harm that they will be brought to if they raise an alarm. This is influenced by the personality type and early childhood grooming. If the risk assessment is low the actions will be more aggressive against such acts, if not it will be the opposite. The other point that influences for many is a quick cost to benefit analysis. What can I gain from raising this? If the quick analysis produces a positive result then the actions that follow are more aggressive, if not, the actions are more subdued. The group dynamics that exists in the company has an important role to play. If the members of the group at the workplace are more cohesive, there will be a stronger response to such incidences, which is a strong deterrent to the aggressors or any other future aggressors. The role of the leadership is critical.

*"Actions of weak leaders are guided by the "whispers" of their followers, while Strong leaders are driven by the dictate of their conviction,"*

*– Capt Tapas Majumdar.*

What is important to note that the action taken by the group and its leadership is critical to reinforce what is 'acceptable' and what is 'not acceptable' behavior. Culture is after all something that the employees feels and experiences.

*"Sexual harassment at the workplace is a culture issue and the needs to be addressed from a culture point of view. Legislations can only support and reinforce, at best it can be a deterrence. Deterrence is important but cannot stand up in isolation. Leaders must stand up to the occasion and be counted"*

*– Capt Tapas Majumdar*

## Chapter 2: Providing for safer workplaces

## aligning to the world effort

The UN Convention on the Elimination of all Forms of Discrimination against Women (CEDAW) was adopted by the UN General Assembly in 1979. India ratified the CEDAW on June 25, 1993, which provides that protection against sexual harassment is universally recognized human right. Often described as an international bill of rights for women, it calls for the equality of women and men in terms of human rights and fundamental freedoms in the political, economic, social, cultural and civil spheres. It underlines that discrimination and attacks on women's dignity violate the principle of equality of rights. Workplace sexual harassment is a form of gender discrimination which violates a woman's fundamental right to equality and right to life, guaranteed under Articles 14, 15 and 21 of the Constitution of India. By passing the Sexual Harassment of Women at Workplace (Prevention, Prohibition and Redressal) Rules, 2013 ("POSH Rules"), the Government of India has fulfilled its obligations under the Convention on the Elimination of all Forms of Discrimination against Women. CEDAW. In January 1992, adopted the General Recommendation No. 19 which recognized the ill effects of sexual harassment at the workplace, and subsequently provided for measures, to be taken by respective states for elimination of such practices. Such practices must be outlawed not only because they result in gender discrimination, but also since they create a hostile work environment, which undermines the dignity, self-esteem and confidence of the female employees, and tends to alienate them.

## A Global Perspective

In the United States of America one of the first cases to be decided by the US Supreme Court, was in the year 1986, i.e. Meritor vs. Vinison, 1986 (477) US. The Congress had enacted Section 703, Title VI of the Civil Rights Act, 1964, to address the issue of sexual harassment at the workplace. The courts in USA have been willing to intervene on a range of issues and complaints, including inadequate response or action by the employer[1], resulting in liability. Thus, it has been ruled in some decisions, Ellison vs. Brady, [1991] 924 F. 872, Fuller vs. City of Oakland, [1995] 47 F. 1522 and Yamaguchi vs. Widnall, [1997] 109 F. 1475, that appropriate remedial and corrective action includes measures reasonably calculated to end current harassment and to deter future harassment from the same or other offenders. In Ellison vs. Brady, [1991] 924 F. 872, the US Court explained the issue of Sexual harassment as, *"We believe that in evaluating the severity and pervasiveness of sexual harassment, we should focus on the perspective of the victim. Courts should consider the victim's perspective and not stereotyped notions of acceptable behavior."*

If we only examined whether a reasonable person would engage in allegedly harassing conduct, we would run the risk of reinforcing the prevailing level of discrimination. Harassers could continue to harass merely because a discriminatory practice was common, and victims of harassment would have no remedy. We therefore prefer to analyse harassment from the victim's perspective. A

---

[1] An employer refers to; The head of the department, organization, undertaking, establishment, enterprise, institution, office, branch or unit of the Appropriate Government or local authority or such officer specified in this behalf. Any person (whether contractual or not) responsible for the management, supervision and control of a designated workplace. A person or a household who employs or benefits from the employment of domestic worker or women employees.

complete understanding of the victim's view requires, among other things, an analysis of the different perspectives of men and women. Conduct that many men consider unobjectionable may offend many women. A male manager might believe, for example, that it is ok for him to tell a female subordinate that she `is looking very attractive in that dress' or `you are dressed to kill today.' The female subordinate, however, may find such comments offensive. Men tend to view some forms of sexual harassment as "harmless social interactions to which only overly-sensitive women would object". The characteristically male view depicts sexual harassment as comparatively harmless amusement.

It is important to understand this that there is a broad range of viewpoints among women as a group, but at the same time many women share common concerns which men do not necessarily share. For example, because women are disproportionately victims of rape and sexual assault, women have a stronger incentive to be concerned with sexual behavior. Women who are victims of mild forms of sexual harassment may understandably worry whether a harasser's conduct is merely a prelude to violent sexual assault. Men, who are rarely victims of sexual assault, may view sexual conduct in a vacuum without a full appreciation of the social setting or the underlying threat of violence that a woman may perceive. In order to shield employers from having to accommodate the characteristic concerns of the rare hyper-sensitive employee, we hold that a aggrieved woman states a prima facie case of hostile environment sexual harassment when she alleges conduct which a reasonable woman would consider sufficiently severe or pervasive to alter the conditions of employment and create an abusive working environment.

Australia has enacted the Sex Discrimination Act 1984, the United Kingdom has enacted the Sex Discrimination Act, 1975, and framed the Sexual Discrimination and Employment Protection (Remedies) Regulations, 1993.

## India's Perspective

A safe workplace is a woman's legal right. A woman's fundamental right to equality and right to life, guaranteed under Articles 14, 15 and 21 of the Constitution of India. These articles ensure a person's right to equal protection under the law, to live a life free from discrimination on any ground and to protection of life and personal liberty. Workplace sexual harassment not only creates an insecure and hostile working environment for women but also impedes their ability to deliver in today's competing world. Apart from interfering with their performance at work, it also adversely affects their social and economic growth and puts them through physical and emotional suffering.

Before 1997, there were no formal guidelines for how an incident involving sexual harassment at workplace should be dealt by an employer. Women experiencing sexual harassment at workplace had to lodge a complaint under Section 354 of the Indian Penal Code that deals with the 'criminal assault of women to outrage women's modesty' and Section 509 that punishes an individual or individuals for using a 'word, gesture or act intended to insult the modesty of a woman'. These sections left the interpretation of 'outraging women's modesty' to the discretion of the investigating agency. Clarity and definitiveness eluded the spirit of the act and this was an important reason why a focused act was required.

India's first legislation specifically addressing the issue of workplace sexual harassment; the Sexual Harassment of Women at Workplace (Prevention, Prohibition and

Redressal) Act, 2013 ("POSH Act") was enacted by the Ministry of Women and Child Development, India in 2013. The Government also subsequently notified the rules under the POSH Act titled the Sexual Harassment of Women at Workplace (Prevention, Prohibition and Redressal) Rules, 2013 ("POSH Rules"). The year 2013 also witnessed the promulgation of the Criminal Law (Amendment) Act, 2013 ("Criminal Law Amendment Act") which has criminalized offences such as sexual harassment, stalking and voyeurism.

Although the law preventing sexual harassment at workplace has been in force since 2013, there remains lack of clarity on various aspects pertaining to the statute, including what constitutes sexual harassment, obligations of an employer, remedies/safeguards available to the victim, procedure of investigation, etc. Many are also not fully aware of the criminal consequences of sexual harassment. Lewd jokes, inappropriate comments etc. are dismissed as normal, with women being hesitant to initiate actions due to apprehension of being disbelieved or ridiculed; which underpins the need for greater awareness and greater enforcement.

# Chapter 3: Model to building a sustainable culture that promotes secure workplace

The model discussed below is proposed as a tool to build a work culture that will promote a secure work culture. The 3 steps in the model define the stages in development of the culture at the workplace.

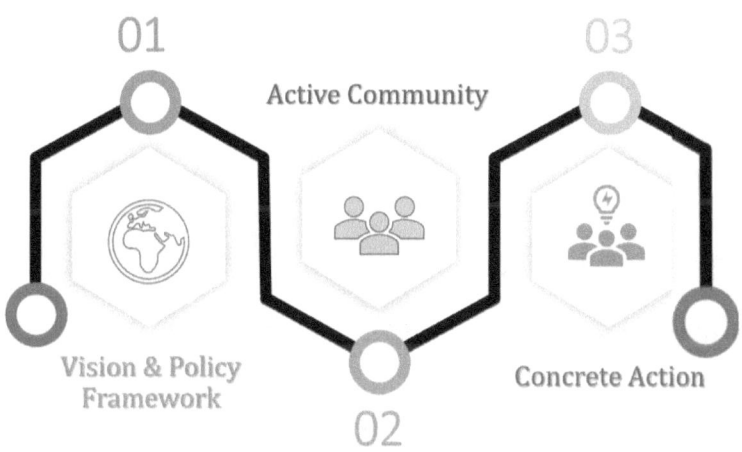

01

Active Community

03

Vision & Policy Framework

Concrete Action

02

3 steps towards building a culture that promotes a secure workplace

The First step can also be referred as defining state and building the framework.

Step 1: Vision & Policy framework

## Vision

A Vision statement is an important statement that clearly sets out the intent, purpose and direction as the top management envisages. The Vision Statement must be bold and audacious. Once displayed it is a strong message that is delivered to all from the top management and it plays an important part as a strong deterrent. This must be supported by a well-defined policy or a framework through which the organization shall follow and achieve the stated vision. This linkage is important. Writing a vision statement is critical and needs to be articulated well to convey the intent of the management in clear and no uncertain terms. Consider the following while drafting your vision statement.

Have a clear picture of the intended outcome. This is the desired state that you want to achieve within a certain period. These must be definitive, avoid using words like 'looking to be', 'should', 'could', 'can be', etc. Instead consider words like 'will be', 'must be' etc. These are action-oriented words and are more definitive and forceful. Avoid writing generic statements that could apply to any company in any field. At the very least, you need to make sure that your vision statement addresses the industry your company exists in. Link your Vision statement to your core values. Identify the values that are core, hence non comprisable for your organization. Relook and reassess, you may need to retain a few elements that currently fulfil your values while also incorporating new elements that can address those values more effectively. Revisit and revalidate. Your vision statement should solve the problem at hand, in this case making the company compliant to the letter and spirit of the Preventions of Sexual Harassment Laws and creating a safer workplace for your employees. Focus on the ideal solution, even if it seems difficult as of now. Let the statement be bold and audacious. It should not be something that you would easily achieve or gives a feel that you are forced to create it; just because the law says so. The vision statement must state the expected output and give a timeframe.

## Policy Framework

A good policy framework gives clarity, creates a sense of definitiveness and accessibility and encourages redressal. It is acts as a deterrent for any and potential aggressor and gives a sense of safety to any potential victim. It comprises of a set of principles and long-term goals that form the basis of making rules and guidelines and gives overall direction to any future course of actions that may be needed to be taken in case of an eventuality. In general, a framework is a real or conceptual structure intended to serve as a support or guide that translates into something meaningful and useful. It lays out the path and boundaries passing through which the vision will be achieved. A framework is designed to ensure that a clear and consistent governance and management approach is adopted that enables and furthers the purpose of the policy in line with the vision and relevant legislative and regulatory requirements. It enables efficient and effective decision making, which provides guidance under variety of eventualities and besides giving clarity on risk mitigation initiatives. It establishes clear accountabilities and delegated authorities for individual roles and groups.

While we are Role, it will be important to note that most policies frameworks define employer's role, employee's role and roles of Internal Complaint Committee, but they miss out an important role i.e. the witnesses or bystanders / colleague or a friend of the victim. Most choose silence, on account of insecurity and the threat of being victimized. Their role and responsibilities must be defined, I say this for two important reasons. Firstly, they have first-hand knowledge and are a potential witness if the matter goes to the Internal Complaint Committee, so they need protection as well. Secondly, by the virtue of being present they are the first line of defence for the victim and need to be empowered. In line with the whistle blower policy, witnesses must be given protection under the policy and also be empowered to act, to prevent the incidence.

## Top Management commitment

Top Management commitment should not just be there but should be visible. The chief executive officer or a senior management representative should endorse the policy and emphasize the fact that all staff are required to comply with it. Officially launch the prevention of sexual harassment policy at a full staff meeting by members of the Top

Management. E-mail copies, that are signed off by the top management, of the policy to employees, put a copy on the intranet and place an automatic shortcut on employee desktops. Provide the policy to new staff as a standard part of induction. Display the policy on notice boards and include it in induction manuals. Ask employees to sign a copy of the policy acknowledging they have received and understood it. Include the policy statement in the appointment letters, thus making it an integral part of the terms and conditions of employment.

**Statement of commitment on prevention of sexual harassment at the workplace.**

A policy on Prevention of Sexual Harassment at the workplace is an important deterrence to any future offender, besides being a reassuring factor for present and future employees. Prevention is the best strategy for eliminating sexual harassment in the workplace. The detailing and advancement of a written policy which makes it clear that sexual harassment will not be tolerated under any circumstances. This is not just about staying compliant to the Law of the Land but going beyond the letter of the law to the spirit of the law. It adds on to the employer brand of an organization, both internally and externally. It reflects upon the culture of the organization and illustrates their will to act against any such violation and create a safe workplace. Hence it is important that the policy truly reflects the will and the intent of the management in no uncertain terms that such violations will be taken seriously and acted upon, besides educating the employees on the complex aspects of Sexual Harassment.

A strong opening statement on the organization's stance on sexual harassment, this should state that the organization is committed to ensuring that the working environment is free from sexual harassment, that it will not be tolerated under any circumstances and that swift disciplinary action will be taken against any employee (or agent) who breaches the policy. To give the policy credibility and maximum impact, the opening statement should appear above the signature of the chief executive officer or managing director. The policy must encourage employees across the organization to create a working environment which is free from sexual harassment and where all members of staff are treated with dignity, courtesy and respect. Give examples of acceptable or expected behaviors and of those behaviors that are not acceptable.

A statement that 'sexual harassment' is against the law should be clearly mentioned. The policy should make it clear that sexual harassment is against the law. Reference should be made to the laws that apply to the organization. Staff need to know that legal action could be taken against them for sexual harassment and that they could also be exposing the company to liability.

As an enabler, the policy must make provision for training of the members of the Internal Complaints Committee (ICC) and a clear approach to raising awareness amongst employees to ensure that all employees know their rights and responsibilities.

**Policy on prevention of sexual harassment at the workplace.**

There is no stated standard content that needs to be included in the policy and that there is no legal requirement on what the content of a policy should include, it is left up to the employer to decide the content of the policy. However, given that the policy is a deterrence initiative, having impact on the culture and employer brand, it is important that the some of the critical aspects are covered in the policy. Some employers incorporate information on prevention of sexual harassment into a general workplace harassment policy which covers other forms of harassment (such as harassment on the grounds of race, disability, sexual preference or age). Others decide there is a need for a standalone prevention of sexual harassment policy, particularly if sexual harassment is a common or recurring problem within the workplace. It is up to employers to decide what is most appropriate for them. In both cases it is important that key aspects of prevention of Sexual Harassment are well-defined and addressed comprehensively. If the policy is too broad or generic its impact and clarity may be compromised.

Policy should reflect the consciousness and commitment of the organization. Organization's culture is a critical ingredient for the success of the policy. Employees who work in your company come from the society at large, and this can be very diverse, value systems may differ, beliefs may contradict. However, research shows that despite the variations it is possible to have a common culture at the workplace. Behaviors that are acceptable or not acceptable can be defined, reinforced and adhered to. It is good to assess the work culture of the company, either formally or informally, before drafting the policy. This will give you vital inputs on possible scenarios in which workplace related harassment can occur and can be assessed and covered. The company should take inputs from the management and employee to identify the needs of the organization and the potential areas of risks that need to be mitigated through the policy.

Policy should dovetail into the way of life of the organization and laydown actions that are acceptable or unacceptable behaviors in line with the philosophy of the organization. The management and managers at all levels should take a consistent stance on sexual harassment considering the act for necessity of compliance with the law and risks. A well-drafted policy articulates a uniform organizational stance enables the employer and his team which is associated with sexual harassment, it leaves little room for inconsistency in the actions of different organizational participants, which is always beneficial.

Cover all essential points in line with the Prevention of Sexual Harassment laws and industry best practices. Your Prevention of Sexual Harassment policy should cover all the essential points required to make a comprehensive policy. Broadly, this must cover Prohibition, Prevention and Redressal. In addition, in cases of listed companies, cover any mandatory disclosures and other requirement. It must have sufficiently detailed points, illustrations or examples which enable your employees to understand the policy in a simple manner. Moreover, the policy should be in line with the provisions of the law. Remember that although, the basic principles of anti-sexual harassment law remain the same throughout the world, and there is no harm in considering the best practices of the industry globally. However, do not adopt the policy of other companies without applying your mind to it. Also, remember it is "Prevention of Sexual Harassment Policy" and NOT "Sexual Harassment Policy".

Keep the policy simple to understand for all sections of employees. The policy will apply to all sections of the employee. Hence it is important to keep the policy simple and must be understood by all sections of your employees. The language should be concise and clear. Give examples where you can. While drafting an effective policy, one should remember that the policy will be uniformly applicable to all the employees, which might include the white and blue-collared workers, in the organization. Simplify using charts and diagrams wherever necessary. If required prepare translated copies of the policy in local language where the office is situated. While translating it keep the language "Conversational" rather than technical, use more of local terms, but define it in the glossary.

## Visual reinforcement of the management commitment to a safer workplace.

A picture speaks a thousand words, this is as valid today as it was valid earlier when the phrase was coined. Visual communication is the art of passing information to people by the use of gestures, images, signs, posters and short films advertisement among others. Visual communication is the most effective way of passing information because the human mind processes things in images. Most people respond quickly to visual images instead of texts. Visual communication breaks the barriers of language, but mind you it does not break the barriers of culture. Some cultures read and write left to right while some other exactly the opposite, while designing visuals, one must be mindful. It saves time, it is easier to process a visual signal quickly than to read a sentence of a paragraph full of text. An image will pass a lot of information within a short a time because one image can have a thousand words. Visual communication improves the clarity of information. When using images to communicate the policy, use simple and clear graphics that will pass the same message to the targeted audience clearly with less or no ambiguity. Leads to better retention of information. Since the human brain processes information in image form, a person will be able to retain visual information for long. People easily forget what they hear or read easily but retain images for long. This is because images are stored in long-term memory, and words and texts are stored in short term memory. It is simple to understand. Even an illiterate person can understand visual communication hence makes it an effective communication method to all. Its simplicity makes it easy for people to understand the information.

Define clearly what is and what is not Sexual Harassment.

Clearly worded definition of sexual harassment is important for clarity. There is no single, universally accepted definition of sexual harassment. However, the definition adopted should be consistent with the legal definition in the POSH Act to avoid any confusion. The most important element to emphasize in any definition is that sexual harassment is unwelcome behavior of a sexual nature. For example, sexual harassment can be defined in the following way.

Sexual harassment is any unwanted, unwelcome or uninvited behavior of a sexual nature which makes a person feel humiliated, intimidated or offended. Sexual harassment can take many different forms and may include physical contact, verbal comments, jokes, propositions, the display of offensive material or other behavior which creates a sexually hostile working environment. Examples of sexual harassment that may be relevant to the working environment. The policy should identify specific examples of sexual harassment, such as, uninvited touching, uninvited kisses or embraces, obscene jokes or comments, making promises or threats in return for sexual favours, displays of sexually graphic material including posters, pinups, cartoons, graffiti or messages left on notice boards, desks or common areas, repeated invitations to go out after prior refusal, exposing genitals or sexual gestures, insults, taunts, teasing or name-calling of a sexual nature, staring or leering at a person or at parts of their body, unwelcome physical contact such as massaging a person without invitation, deliberately brushing up against them or forcing a person to perform sexual acts, touching or fiddling with a person's clothing including lifting up skirts or shirts, flicking bra straps, or putting hands in a person's pocket, requests for sex, sexually explicit conversation, persistent questions or insinuations about a person's private life, offensive phone calls or letters, stalking, offensive e-mail messages or computer screen savers, to name a few.

Similarly, clearly distinguish what does not constitute sexual harassment. The policy should explain that sexual harassment is not behavior which is based on mutual attraction, friendship and respect. If the interaction is consensual, welcome and reciprocated it is not sexual harassment.

**Strategy to achieve a safer workplace and desired outcomes**

It is desirable that a clear strategy is adopted, and an awareness is provisioned for in the policy. Employees must know who the management is planning to achieve its vision on making the workplace safe. The key strategy must include, Clear, unambiguous Complain and Investigation Procedure. A clear unambiguous complaint procedure creates awareness and reinforces confidence of the employees. It is an evidence to the company's compliance to the relevant laws of the land and to the stated vision of the management.

## Step 2 Active Community

Given that Sexual Harassment is linked to culture and that

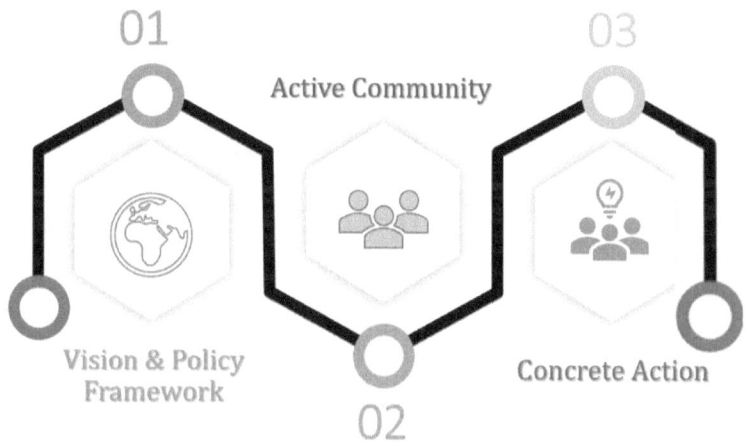

3 steps towards building a culture that promotes a secure workplace

Active community is a resultant of the culture that prevails in the organization. The degree of activism and freedom of expression and action is a direct resultant of the norms that prevail in the culture. Culture is the key determinant, creating the right culture is the key. Culture may be understood as, a set of common understandings expressed in language, values, beliefs, expectations that members come to share and have a well-organized system of reinforcing them.

Broadly culture can be divided into cognitive and normative. The cognitive component is the foundation of social behavior. It defines and guides the behavior of the members in the culture. It holds the values and beliefs from which emanates the acceptable and not-acceptable behavior. This is passed on from generation to generations as the way of life. The normative behavior encompasses the translation of cognitive component of culture into specifics of behavior, way of thinking, norms (rules). These are practiced as traditions; morality and it defines the expected behavior and interactions within the members of the culture. Simplistically put, culture is cultivating a pattern. Patterns in values, norms, traditions and reinforcing them. This pattern creates uniqueness that differentiates one culture from the other.

## Values

Values and value systems form a very important part of culture. Values may be adopted or would have evolved over a period within the organization. It guides behavior in all situations and helps in standardization of behavior within a culture and gives a sense of right and wrong. It represents the degree of importance that the culture attaches to the behavior. In an organization core values are generally non-negotiable, and they evolve over a much longer period, while non-core values evolve over relatively shorter period.

Value system on the other hand is a more agile and reactive system. The output of this system are values. It is a continuous process of interacting with the external and internal environment (business and societal) in which the organization operates and learns through continuous application of the current values. Changes in the environment may translate into adoption of different values, that is compatible with the environment and the core values of the organization. Let me explain this through an example. During the industrial revolution, the divide between Management and Labour was significant. Loosely speaking, it was the exploiter and exploited. Management put in place rules that met their requirement with scanty regards to labour health, safety and welfare. This changed over a period with the rise of trade union activism. Today we talk about prevention of modern-day slavery and being an equal opportunity employer. This transformation has happened as the organizations operating in their respective environments have adapted to their environment, resulting in changes in value. Today many organizations have 'equal opportunity employer' as part of their core values.

This transformation happens over a period and can broadly be understood to undergo 3 stages. Change confrontation, Solutioning & Solution Implementation and Adoption of a new or renewed value.

Change confrontation: People in the culture continuously engage with the environment (business or societal). The existing values are applied that reflects in the behavior of individual members. However, the environment is also evolving on a continuous basis. The business environment is impacted by multitude of external factors. Some that it creates itself, like disruptive innovation, and some that is not in its control, like government legislations. Societal environment also is influenced on a continuous basis, like multicultural work force that brings together different value systems within the organization. These changes threaten the existing status quo, hence is faced with resistance, both active and passive. Beyond a threshold the change is confronted and debated. This is the storming phase, where the clash of the old and the prospective new values take place. This debates and discussions are important for the new to take shape.

Solutioning & Solution Implementation: This is a follow up of the change confrontation phase. Having bottomed out and accepted that the change needs to be responded to in earnestness, in this phase the members look for solutions. There may not be just one solution, but many. The normal tendency will be to impact the existing systems at the minimum yet accommodating the required change. Behaviors get recalibrated and there is a will to experiment to check if the response is adequate to accommodate the change.

Adoption: Of the solutions tried by the members the one that works and achieves the desired goals is then adopted. The norms within the members are revised and there is a consensus towards achieving them. This is the new normal and any deviation from this exerts peer pressure to comply.

**Norms and Traditions**

Traditions represent a critical piece of our culture. They help form the structure and foundation of our families and our society. They remind us that we are part of a piece of history that defines our past, shapes who we are today and who we are likely to become. Once we ignore the meaning of our traditions, we're in danger of damaging the underpinning of our identity.

Tradition contributes a sense of comfort and belonging. It brings families together and enables people to reconnect with friends. It reinforces values such as freedom, faith, integrity, a good education, personal responsibility, a strong work ethic, and the value of being selfless. Tradition provides a forum to showcase role models, principles and celebrate the things that really matter in life. And above all, tradition offers an excellent context for meaningful pause and reflection.

Contrary to many beliefs, traditions have reasons as to why they exist. There may be scientific and non-scientific in nature, or sometimes even belief based and also logic based. Let me explain this with some examples.

In India, why you should not to sleep with your head towards North? Myth is that it invites ghost or death, but science says that it is because human body has its own magnetic field (Also known as hearts magnetic field, because the flow of blood) and Earth is a giant magnet. When we sleep with head towards north, our body's magnetic field become completely asymmetrical to the Earth's Magnetic field. That cause problems related to blood pressure and our heart needs to work harder in order to overcome this asymmetry of Magnetic fields. Apart from this another reason is that our body have significant amount of iron in our blood. When we sleep in this position, iron from the whole body starts to congregate in brain. This can cause headache, Alzheimer's Disease, Cognitive Decline, Parkinson disease and brain degeneration.

While having dinner / lunch, we start with spice & and end with sweet? Our ancestors have stressed on the fact that our meals should be started off with something spicy and sweet dishes should be taken towards the end. The significance of this eating practice is that while spicy things activate the digestive juices and acids and ensure that the digestion process goes on smoothly and efficiently, sweets or carbohydrates pulls down the digestive process. Hence, sweets were always recommended to be taken as a last item.

Building and reinforcing traditions are a must for an effective culture.

## Building an Active Community

An active community is a strong foundation for creating a safer workplace. It also acts as a strong deterrent and the success of which is important to imbibing a sexual harassment free workplace in the organization's DNA. Your company will benefit from creating and maintaining an active community within the workplace. When you build community, you form an enduring foundation for your business. This foundation influences all aspects of your organization and not goes beyond creating safer workplaces, to include customer experience, Dynamics within employees and with suppliers and customers alike and builds trust. These attributes ultimately affect the success of your brand.

Employee's participation is a key determinant to the success of Active Community. If I may be more specific, employee's "Willing" participation is the key to success.

The willing participation comes when the company creates an environment that makes the employees feel welcomed, valued and it adds a strong sense of purpose. The community needs to have influence, even if limited, on the objectives that the company has assigned, it may or may not have the power to enforce but must be heard on merit and considered seriously for implementation.

An individual's physical surroundings, or what scientists call "built environments," have a large influence on his or her level of activity. This starts with the foundation which are the stated vision and values that has been discussed earlier. Strengthen the foundation with your company policies like the policy on prevention of sexual harassment. Keep learning from incidences and changes happening in the internal and external environment. Constitute employee advisory groups or welfare groups to study their impact, create awareness and if required recommend changes to the policy. This is the right forum to ensure inclusivity and diversity. Engage with employees across all sections including age, education, sex, sexual preference, although I am not a advocate of reservations, but do it is you must.

**Build the right foundations.**

Start with the three critical factors for your foundation. Start with your vision statement. It should, in no uncertain terms, convey the intent, purpose and direction of the management with regards to prevention of sexual harassment at the workplace. Let the statement be bold and audacious and display the signed copy at prominent places. In continuation of this should be your values. Values guides behavior in all situations and helps in standardization of behavior within a culture and gives a sense of right and wrong. Thirdly is your policy on prevention of sexual harassment. It is important that the Vision Statement,

Values and the Policy be displayed prominently at locations that will visually reinforce the commitment of the management.

## Influencing the Value Systems within your organization on a continuous basis

Look to influence the value systems periodically, this will channelize the positive energy in the desired direction. By creating positive interactions, the learnings will be more constructive. The influencers to the value systems are both internal and external. Reinforce both in a planned and consistent manner.

Some of the key external influencers include, create community champions at workplaces and empower them to closely interact with especially the external environment, like Industry interaction, participating in seminars, being a speaker / panellist in events related to prevention of sexual harassment and creating safer workplaces etc

Internal influencers can include, skill training for current and potential Internal Complaints Committee members, Social bonding initiatives like community service, Updates on the latest developments relating to prevention of sexual harassment, welfare forums, reserved space in company newsletter to engage employees.

Encourage open and frank discussions. Do not shy away from a frank discussion and let the superior logic prevail. Reward and recognise achievements and extraordinary acts that reflect the company values and further the cause of creating safer workplaces.

While discussions are good to have it is the actions that speak the loudest. Focus on actions more rather than argument.

# Step 3: Concrete Action

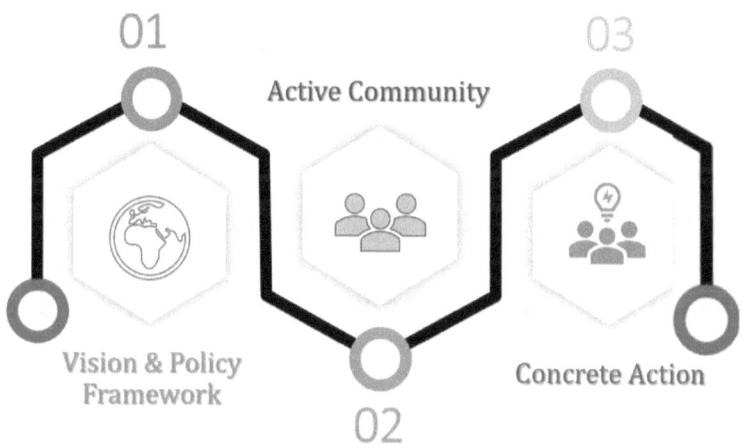

01

Active Community

03

Vision & Policy
Framework

Concrete Action

02

3 steps towards building a culture that promotes a
secure workplace

Concrete and decisive actions speak louder than words. It is a true reflection of the intent that the management carries. It inspires confidence and build trust in the management and the policy and other initiative. It assures the employees that the initiatives and policies are not cosmetic in nature. It is important that the action taken by the management through its established institutions like the Internal Complaints Committee, or the welfare and other social groups is seen. Routing the actions through these institutions ensures the participations of key employees who are influencers of employee opinions and converting them to ambassadors of the cause.

Concrete action is about disciplined implementation, it is the phase between a decision and its realization. It is the vital ingredient between planning and execution. Implementation always occurs according to a fixed pattern. Random implementation can prove counterproductive and inject seeds of bias and other negative influences in the employees, there by impacting the credibility of the action and intent. Effective implementation overcomes the gaps between intention and promise, aspirations, achievement and performance, and prescription and reality. Implementation comprises the ability to achieve specified ends by chosen means.

Once implementation dynamics are set in motion, they become vulnerable to adverse or diversionary views / forces which pull them away from their original design. Hence, a participative implementation approach that is included in the policy will be necessary to move from the realm of intention to the ambit of reality.

Concrete actions based on a predefined and structured manner will carry more credibility. I recommend that concrete actions must be based on the following 4 pillars.

- Principles

- Consistency

- Well informed actions &

- Decisiveness

## Principles

Concrete actions must be based on principles. These principles must be non-comprisable and uniformly applied regardless of the individuals involved. Key amongst them is Procedural Fairness.

## Procedural Fairness

Procedural fairness is concerned with the procedures used by a decision maker, rather than the actual outcome reached. It requires a fair and proper procedure be used when deciding. 'Procedural fairness' means acting fairly in administrative decision making. It relates to the fairness of the procedure by which a decision is made, and not the fairness in a substantive sense of that decision. The idea of procedural fairness in the processes that resolve disputes and allocate resources towards achieving this goal. It ensures transparency and meets the "Rights" of the accused to a fair hearing, although this applies to both the accused and the aggrieved woman. It broadly consists of following well documented procedure. The procedure for a concrete action on charges of sexual harassment must be well documented and be made available to employees. This procedure must be followed as a general approach, any changes could be more circumstantial but be justified.

A hearing appropriate to the circumstances: All parties the issues at hand must be given an opportunity to reply in a way that is appropriate for the circumstances. The accused should not and cannot be forced to indict themselves. They, especially the accused, must be provided with all the relevant information for them to reply to charges and be received and considered before the decision is made.

Lack of bias: The concrete action taken as per the declared procedure must be free of bias. This should not just happen but also appear to happen to any reasonable person not connected with the issue at hand.

Full and complete application of mind to the evidence presented to support a decision: All evidences produced by the accused and the aggrieved woman must be thoroughly examined. Those sitting in judgement bears the burden of detailing and applying their minds to the evidences and arrive at reasonable conclusions.

**Principles of Natural Justice & Wednesbury principle**

The basic motive of principle of natural justice is to ensure fairness and also safeguard individual liberty against the arbitrary action. Natural justice encourages equity, fairness and equality. In the concept of common law, natural justice constitutes higher procedural principles introduced by the courts. These principles must guide every judicial, quasi-judicial and administrative procedures. Principles of natural justice includes:

- Nemo in propria causa judex, esse debet - No one should be made a judge in his own case, or the rule against bias. The rule against bias flows from following two principles: -

  o No one should be a judge in his own cause

  o Justice should not only be done but manifestly and undoubtedly be seen to be done.

- Audi alteram partem - Hear the other party, or the rule of fair hearing, or the rule that no one should be condemned unheard. This rule covers steps in administrative adjudication starting from notice to final determination. Right to fair hearing thus includes: -

- o Right to notice
- o Right to present case and evidence
- o Right to rebut adverse evidence
- o Right to cross examination
- o Right to legal representation
- o Disclosure of evidence to party
- o Report of enquiry to be shown to the other party
- o Reasoned decisions or speaking orders
- o Rule against bias. This includes personal bias, pecuniary bias, departmental bias or preconceived notion bias.

Reasoned Decision this is linked to the Wednesbury Principle. If the investigation and the conclusion is so outrageous in its defiance of logic or accepted moral standards that no sensible person who had applied his mind to the question to be decided could have arrived at it, then that would make them liable to be quashed on judicial review. The procedure must provide for review / appeal against a decision by the accused. Those sitting in judgement must be consciously aware of this and ensure that while dealing with complaints and the investigations on matter does not contravene the Wednesbury unreasonableness principle.

## Well informed actions

Concrete actions to be meaningful and impactful must emanate from Knowledge and not individual sense of 'Right' and 'Wrong'. Sexual Harassment cases are very sensitive in nature and needs to be dealt with carefully. Little or half knowledge will be counterproductive. To start with a carefully written policy must be well read and understood from an implementation point. The policy should be detailed enough to give a clear picture to those who hold the burden of implementation of the policy. The scope for assumptions and interpretations must be low. It is also important to give a serious thought on those who are tasked with the implementation of the policy. All such employees must be trained well especially in the art of implementation, listening skills, conflict resolution negotiations skills and other skills that are deemed important. They must be trained or be knowledgeable on the legal social impact of the policy. They must have good knowledge of the relevant laws (POSH Act, in case of India). They must have the credentials in the eyes of the accused, the aggrieved woman and with the rest of the population as well.

Concrete action does not always mean immediate loud action. It can be scuttle but timely. Those who are responsible for the implementation of the policy must have the maturity, besides the knowledge, to make a fair judgement on the gravity of the situation and the possible fall out. It is equally important to understand the work culture within the organization. They must be thoughtful in their actions and careful in their conduct.

## Decisiveness

Concrete actions must be decisive in nature. There has to an unwavering effort to close out cases and that there should be no unreasonable delays. There should be visible attempt to delay beyond stipulated period. Decisions must be timely and yet balanced. This does not imply that the process is hastened that it violates either the principles of natural justice. It is important to always remember that the accused is not guilty until proved to be guilty, at the same time, the aggrieved woman should have a sense of reassurance that the management is taking the matter seriously and that her complaint is being address proactively.

## Consistency

The time factor is critical; however, in an attempt to rush up and make a point, arbitrary actions must be avoided. Consistency in dealing with any such complaints gives a sense of clarity, makes the process transparent and predictable. It also treats all cases, regardless of who is involved, equally. The policy document should be the basis of attaining consistency. However, it may not be practically possible to envisage all situations and incorporate them into the policy. There can be contingent situations that needs to be take care of.

Contingencies impacts implementation in several ways hence interactive and active communication channels are important to minimize the discrepancy between what actually is the stated procedure and what you are faced with. The role of external and internal experts will be critical in such cases.

# Chapter 4: Developing a robust complaint procedure that evolves from the Policy Framework

Develop and publish complaints procedures to suit your workplace. The most effective complaint procedures for large organizations offer a range of options for dealing with sexual harassment. Smaller organizations may not have capacity to offer a range of options, but as a minimum should ensure that managers have the knowledge and training to deal with sexual harassment complaints. Most organizations encourage the aggrieved woman to raise the issue with their immediate supervisor, or another manager if the supervisor is the alleged harasser. In smaller organizations there may only be one manager, but in a larger organization the complainant can report the situation to another manager, an Equal Employment Opportunity officer, Human Resources or Industrial Relations manager. The policy must provide for a procedure that is suitable to the organization keeping in mind the sensitivity of the complaint. Direct access to the Top management must be considered.

Sexual harassment complaints frequently involve sensitive or embarrassing information and in some cases an individual may be reluctant to discuss the details with the management hierarchy. Given this sensitivity and the prevalence of sexual harassment against women, this model is unlikely to be suitable if the management hierarchy is predominantly male. It may also be difficult for a person to make a complaint to management if the alleged harasser is part of the chain of responsibility. The approach also depends on supervisors and managers at all levels possessing the necessary complaints handling skills and knowledge about sexual harassment. Organizations may overcome some of these difficulties by designating employees as sexual harassment complaints officers having direct reporting to the Chairwoman of ICC or the Board of Directors. This could be the human resources manager or other nominated management representatives. Complaints authority must be selected based on their skills, experience and sensitivity. They take an active role in the resolution of complaints and should have relatively senior status in the organization to ensure that their role is respected, and they can operate with the necessary level of authority. Contracting out formal complaints' procedures to professional consultants, may be an effective way of dealing with complaints as it promotes the objectivity of the procedures.

## Informal complaint procedures

The policy must provide for informal procedure to deal with complaints of sexual harassment. Informal procedures emphasize resolution rather than factual proof or substantiation of a complaint. Informal ways of dealing with sexual harassment can include the following actions.

The individual who has been harassed wants to deal with the situation themselves but may seek advice on possible strategies from their supervisor or another officer such as the Chairwoman of the ICC or human resource personnel. The individual who has been harassed asks their supervisor to speak to the alleged harasser on their behalf. The supervisor privately conveys the individual's concerns and reiterates the organisation's sexual harassment policy to the alleged harasser without assessing the merits of the case. A complaint is made, the harasser admits the behavior, investigation is not required, and the complaint is resolved through conciliation or counselling of the harasser. A supervisor or manager at the workplace[2] (or Extended

---

[2] A 'workplace' is defined as "any place visited by the employee arising out of or during the course of employment, including transportation provided by the employer for undertaking such a journey." As per this definition, a workplace covers both the organized and un-organized sectors. It also includes all workplaces whether owned by Indian or foreign company having a place of work in India. As per the Act, workplace includes; Government organizations, including, Government company, corporations and cooperative societies;

Workplace[3]) observes unacceptable conduct occurring and takes independent action even though no complaint has been made.

Informal action is usually appropriate where the allegations are of a less serious nature but the individual alleging the behavior wants it to cease, nonetheless. Or the individual alleging the behavior wishes to pursue an informal resolution. Or the parties are likely to have ongoing contact with one another and the complainant wishes to pursue an informal resolution so that the working relationship can be sustained. An employee should not be required to exhaust informal attempts at resolution before formal action commences. Employees have the right to

---

Private sector organizations, venture, society, trust, NGO or service providers etc. providing services which are commercial, vocational, educational, sports, professional, entertainment, industrial, health related or financial activities, including production, supply, sale, distribution or service; Hospitals/Nursing Homes; - Sports Institutes/Facilities; Places visited by the employee (including while on travel) including transportation provided by employer; A dwelling place or house.

[3] 'extended workplace.' In addition to the office of the employer or employee, any place visited by the employee arising out of or during employment, including transportation provided by the employer for the purpose of commuting to and from the place of employment, will also constitute a workplace. Further, social settings endorsed or financed by the employer are also considered a workplace

formalize their complaint or approach an external agency, such as the Local Complaints Committee or any appointed body at any stage.

## Formal complaint procedures

Formal procedures focus on proving whether a complaint is substantiated. They usually involve, investigation of the allegations, application of the principles of procedural fairness, making a finding as to whether the harassment occurred, submitting a report with a recommended course of action to the appropriate decision-maker, implementation of an appropriate outcome.

Formal procedures are usually appropriate where informal attempts at resolution have failed, the complaint involves serious allegations of misconduct and informal resolution could compromise the rights of the parties, the complaint is against a more senior member of staff, the person alleging sexual harassment also alleges victimization, the allegations are denied, the person who claims to have been harassed wishes to proceed and investigation is required to substantiate the complaint, the person alleging sexual harassment wishes to make a formal complaint.

To ensure consistency and fairness, employers should document the steps involved in a formal complaint and clearly inform the parties about the processes involved in considering a complaint in advance. This normally involves a sequence of events that includes, the complainant being is interviewed, and the allegations are recorded in detail, in writing, the allegations are conveyed to the alleged harasser in full, the alleged harasser is given the opportunity to respond and defend themselves against the allegations, if there is a dispute over facts, statements from any witnesses and other relevant evidence are gathered, relevant allegations made during the investigation are made known to both the complainant and alleged harasser, with an opportunity to respond, finding are made as to whether the complaint has substance, written report documenting the investigation process, the evidence, the finding and a recommended outcome/s is submitted to the decision-maker. the decision-maker implements the recommended outcome/s or decides on an alternative course of action.

## The prescribed procedure

There must be a clearly worded prescribed procedure. The content that must cover the complaint and timelines, description of the incident, respondent's name (against whom the complaint is being raised), date and time, working relationship with the person against whom the complaint is being raised, the person designated to manage the workplace sexual harassment complaint is required to provide assistance in writing of the complaint if the complainant seeks it for any reason, written complaints (6 copies) along with supporting documents and names and addresses of witnesses have to be filed within 3 months of the date of the incident. Timeline extendable by another 3 months. Upon receipt of the complaint, 1 copy of the complaint is to be sent to the respondent within 7 days. Upon receipt of the copy of complaint, the respondent is required to reply to the complaint along with a list of supporting documents, and names and addresses of witnesses within 10 working days. The Inquiry must be completed within a total of 90 days from the receipt of the complaint. The Inquiry report must be issued within 10 days from the date of completion of inquiry. The employer is required to act on the recommendations of the ICC within 60 days of receipt of the Inquiry report. Appeal against the decision of the committee is allowed within 90 days from the date of the decision

# Complaints Committee

An effective Complaints Committee is a strong message and a concrete step towards zero tolerance towards any sexual harassment incidences at the workplace. The Act provides for two kinds of complaints mechanisms: Internal Complaints Committee (ICC) and Local Complaints Committee (LCC). All Complaints Committees must have 50 per cent representation of women. ICC or LCC members will hold their position not exceeding three years from the date of their nomination or appointment.

Dealing with workplace sexual harassment complaints is often complex. Hence Complaints Committee/s must possess critical skills, knowledge and capability to effectively carry out their role. That includes sound grasp of the Act, Vishaka Guidelines, applicable Service Rules, relevant laws and an understanding of workplace sexual harassment and related issues. Complaints Committee skills must include an ability to analyse information and reach objective conclusions. They should also be able to communicate effectively, write clearly, listen actively and conduct interviews. They should be competent at showing empathy, being impartial and being thorough. They should be able to identify sexual harassment and its impact. A Complaints Committee is required to be trained to carry out a fair and informed inquiry into a complaint of workplace sexual harassment. An absence of such training will lead to unequal and unfair results, which can cost employers, employees, complainants as well as respondents.

**Constitution of the Internal Complaints Committee (ICC)**

Every employer is obliged to constitute an ICC through a written order. ICC is mandatory. The employee has a fundamental right to a workplace free of sexual harassment. If a woman complains about sexual harassment, given that the company had compiled to the Vishaka Guidelines and set up such a Complaints Committee, the preventative benefit would have ensured a forum where the women employees could seek redress. The availability of such a forum will send a clear message to the workplace that such complaints would be enquired into by a specially designated committee with external expertise and Prevented a series of litigation that followed.

The ICC will be composed of the following members:

- Chairperson Woman: Chairperson Women working at senior level as employee; if not available then nominated from another office/units/ department/ workplace of the same employer

- Members (minimum 2) From amongst employees committed to the cause of women/ having legal knowledge/experience in social work

- External Member from amongst NGO/associations committed to the cause of women or a person familiar with the issue of Sexual Harassment Where the office or administrative units of a workplace are in different places, division or sub-division, an ICC has to be set up at every administrative unit and office.

- Not less than half of the ICC Members shall be women. The term of the ICC Members shall not exceed 3 years. A minimum of 3 Members of the ICC including the Presiding Officer are to be present for conducting the inquiry.

**External Members on the Complaints Committee/s**

The Act refers to external members, which generally means persons who have expertise with the issue of sexual harassment. Given the largely intangible nature of workplace sexual harassment, there are a range of complexities involved in responding effectively to workplace sexual harassment complaints. For this reason, external third party/ members on the Complaints Committee/s (from civil society or legal background) should possess attributes like, demonstrated knowledge, skill and capacity in dealing with workplace sexual harassment issues/complaints; sound grasp and practice of the legal aspects/implications. Such expertise will greatly benefit Complaints Committees in terms of fair and informed handling of complaints to lead to sound outcomes. These external third-party members shall be paid for their services on the Complaints Committees as prescribed.

A 'person familiar with issues relating to women' would mean such persons who have expertise in issues related to sexual harassment and may include, at least 5 years of experience as a social worker, working towards women's empowerment and, addressing workplace sexual harassment; Familiarity with labour, service, civil or criminal law

## Guiding approach

The principles of Natural Justice must always be followed by the ICC in the procedure followed for inquiry. In case the ICC does not follow the principles of Natural Justice, its findings and the report prepared may be set aside. In India, the concepts of social and economic justice that can be seen in the Preamble of the Constitution are based on the principles of natural justice. Article 311 incorporates many of the features of the natural justice without explicitly mentioning it. Violation of natural justice is equal to violation of Equality of the Article 14. It is a higher procedural principle developed by the courts, which every judicial, quasi-judicial and administrative agency must follow while taking any decision adversely affecting the rights of a private individual. Natural justice implies fairness, equity and equality. The clear and consistent position of the courts has always been that the courts do not sit as appellate bodies over the findings and conclusions of departmental authorities. The only instance that may merit interference is when there has been a violation of natural law principles. However, in case the very nature of the body constituted is considered vitiated, an inquiry can be ordered to be conducted afresh. Further, many judicial pronouncements have helped in chalking out certain specific circumstances where it may be concluded that natural law principles have been violated and have been given greater legitimacy by Section 11 of the Act that provides for the opportunity to be heard and to make representations against findings to both parties; as well as by Rule 7 of the rules framed thereunder which expressly lay down that an inquiry must be conducted in accordance with the principles of natural justice. Several judgements on the matter have quoted the foundational E.P Royappa judgement to emphasize the indispensability of fairness and absence of arbitrariness in the workings of the Internal Complaint Committees.

In following the principles of natural justice, the ICC must make sure that the fair opportunity given to the person against whom the complaint is made must be seen considering maintaining an atmosphere where the complainant may freely express their grievance.

An April 2017 judgement by the Kerala High Court in L.S. Sibu v. Air India comprehensively laid down that ICC's must follow the principles of natural justice in conducting their enquiry. The case involved a complaint by 17 Air India-Singapore Air Transport Services against an Officer-Apron. While the officer claimed he had not been given the right to cross examine witnesses, the Air India authorities contended that it was merely a preliminary enquiry and hence, further disciplinary action would be initiated where he may defend any action proposed. A very important position it clarifies, is that natural justice principles are elastic and depend upon the context. The fundamental principle of natural justice is that when a prejudicial statement is made against someone it shall not be used against him until he has been given an opportunity to contradict and correct. In a sexual harassment case, fair opportunity must be understood in the context of free expression of grievance. Thus, the court held that since verbal cross examination is not the only measure available, the Committee may undertake any other such measure if the aggrieved is feeble and may not be able to withstand cross examination. Thus, while acknowledging the paramountcy of natural justice principles, this recent ruling has also allowed for acknowledgement of alternatives to rigid standards such as a requirement for verbal cross-examination, thereby extending much needed protection to the aggrieved.

Again, in August 2017, the Delhi High Court in Ashok Kumar Singh v. University of Delhi, taking note of the aforementioned judgement, the court acknowledged the need to ensure a balanced view of natural justice in the proceedings of the ICC and gave directions to the ICC to carry out its enquiry meaningfully and expeditiously. It allowed, therefore, in view of the condition of the witnesses and complainant, that the witnesses may be allowed to remain anonymous and answer cross-examination questions through a questionnaire. This reflects the judicial understanding of the equally pressing need to ensure that witnesses or complainants are not intimidated in the process of ensuring natural justice to the person against whom the case is filed. As in the case, a period of two years had already passed between the filing of the complaint and preparation of the report, the court forcefully re-emphasized that an enquiry must be completed within ninety days of receipt of the complaint. The court issued instructions to the ICC on how to conduct the enquiry in the specific case, including instructions to submit the report within three months and start the enquiry in two weeks, considering the delay.

This case represents a conciliation of two stances whereby the court is not merely detached observer but can interfere only if the demand is urgent.

The ICC need not mechanically issue notices on receipt of a complaint, it may apply its mind to the facts and circumstances to determine the merits of the case.

In 2014, the Calcutta High Court in Shri Debdulal Maity v. National Insurance Company , held that the scheme of the Act does not require the committee to mechanically issue a notice upon receipt of a complaint.

The Internal Complaints Committee must apply its mind to determine whether a complaint relates to a sexual harassment as defined under the Act of 2013 and whether an incident of sexual harassment occurred at the workplace. It is only based on such prima facie findings that it may attempt conciliation under Section 10 or begin an inquiry under Section 11.

There must be no bias or undue influence in the workings of the ICC and the members must be impartial.

Linda Eastwood v. Union of India is the best illustration of vitiated ICC proceedings and became a formative case on the subject. the complainant had been working in a company (GOI Undertaking) , for 33 years. She issued a complaint against the Mr XYZ alleging sexual harassment over a period of two years and the matter was referred to the ICC. During the investigation, some members of the ICC were shifted and hence, unable to continue in the capacity of members. The first committee unanimously felt that a prima facie case had been made out, but the final report was signed only by the Chairperson of the committee. This report, which was duly sent to the concerned authorities concluded that the charges were proven and that he must be punished under the provisions of the law- but no action was taken. In the meantime, the respondent was appointed the CMD and reconstituted a committee that included some members who had been a part of the old committee. This committee came to a different conclusion, that the respondent had erred in using impolite language to the complainant on occasion and that this was being used to implicate him on false sexual harassment charges. The court held that the reports neither of the Internal Complaints Committees could be relied upon, as the first was not representative of the collective will and the second had been appointed by the accused himself, clearly violating the principle of natural justice. A de novo enquiry was ordered. The basic principles that must be ensured, thus, are that the procedure followed must be fair and unbiased, there must be no undue influence from a senior level and the selection of the members of the committee must be free of any blemish.

The ICC must allow the respondent the right to challenge any prejudicial statements made against them, allow them the right to cross examine the complainant and witnesses, as well as lead evidence in their favor.

In Manjeet Singh v. Indraprastha Gas, the Delhi High Court held that the principles of natural justice would include an opportunity for cross-examination; interpreting the term broadly to ensure that the right is not just nominally extended but ensured. In support of its conclusions, it drew a parallel to the complaint committees created under the Vishaka guidelines which were to function in accordance with the Civil Services Conduct Rules and whereby actions by the disciplinary authority could only be taken in accordance with the rules. Thus, in this instant case, the preparation of a list of questions could not be considered a grant of the right to cross examine-as unlike verbal questioning, there would be no ability to reformulate the question or draw cohesive conclusions. Accordingly, the order was struck down. Similarly, if the respondent is not given the right to lead evidence in their own favour, the entire enquiry becomes wholly one sided and fails to abide by the natural justice principle of granting both sides a fair hearing, hence, rendering such an enquiry vitiated. Similarly, the Delhi High Court in Avinash Mishra v Union of India[6], struck down a report in keeping with natural justice principles as the accused had not been not been given the opportunity to cross examine witnesses or provided with copies of their statements. The inquiry then had to be conducted afresh from the stage of examination of witnesses, as this part of it had been vitiated.

The ICC has the sole jurisdiction to inquire into the complaints that come to it and its findings can only be set aside if the order is shockingly disproportionate.

However, while in the aforementioned instances the court intervened to prevent contravention of natural justice, the Bombay High Court judgement in Vidya Akhave v. Union of India makes explicit the fact that the court must not ordinarily interfere in the proceedings of ICCs. In this case, the employee made a complaint against her immediate supervisor and thereafter, sought the establishment of an Internal Complaints Committee as legally mandated. Post this, the committee was set up and on the basis of its report, the Disciplinary authority demoted the supervisor by two ranks, lowered the pay-scale in accordance, and transferred him to another city. The employee challenged the validity of this order under Section 226, claiming that the punishment was disproportionate. Here, the court declined to give an order interfering with the decision of the committee, emphasising that judicial restraint must be exercised regarding exercise of powers under Article 226. An order of the Internal Complaints Committee, therefore, can only be interfered with if the order is shockingly disproportionate. Interference is only warranted if there is noncompliance with the principles of international law, if it is against the Wednesbury principle in such that (a) the Order was contrary to law, (b) relevant factors were not considered, (c) irrelevant factors were considered and (d) no reasonable person would have taken such a decision and if it contrary to the doctrine of proportionality. If an enquiry is fair and proper, and all evidence and witness statements were duly considered; the court is not entitled to give a second opinion merely because it has the legal authority to do so. Thus, this judgement greatly raised the stature of ICC's in that their independence and decision-making power were given paramount consideration.

Enquiry made by the ICC is a full-fledged inquiry as to finding of fact and not merely a preliminary inquiry.

In the L.S.Sibu vs Air India case, the court held that inquiry under Section 13 of the Act is clearly a full fledged inquiry as to finding of fact. Thus, the status of the ICC is that of an Inquiry Committee for disciplinary action under the Service Rules. Further, under Section 15, the ICC can provide for the compensation to be paid by the delinquent to the aggrieved. Recognizing the appellate remedy available under Section 18, the Court drew the conclusion that this proved that the inquiry report is final unless appealed and cannot be subsequently varied by the employer through follow up action under Section 13.

**The Internal Complaints Committee is mandated to come to a definite conclusion as to guilt.**

In the Ashok Kumar case, the petitioner contested, in addition to the fact that principles of natural justice had not been followed, that all the three reports prepared by the ICC contained only prima facie findings and hence, must be set aside. The court, upon a perusal of the relevant sections, found that an inquiry is always initiated under Section 11 of the Act; and after the inquiry by the ICC, submitted to the employer under Section 13; and hence, such inquiry is not merely a preliminary inquiry.

**General guideline to conducting an enquiry**

Any aggrieved woman may make, in writing, a complaint of sexual harassment at work place to the ICC, within a period of three months from the date of incident and in case of a series of incidents, within a period of three months from the date of last incident. 6 copies of a written complaint should be submitted to the Committee or any of its members along with list of witnesses and supporting documents. Additional documents and list of witnesses can be submitted to ICC at a later stage during the proceeding. Provided that where such complaint cannot be made in writing, the Presiding Officer or any other member of the ICC shall render all reasonable assistance to the woman for making the complaint in writing. Provided further that the ICC for the reasons to be recorded in writing, can extend the time limit not exceeding three months, if it is satisfied that the circumstances were such which prevented the woman from filing a complaint within the said period.

Any complaint received by the members should be immediately forwarded to the Presiding Officer, and this must be notified to other committee members at the earliest and not later than 3 days and a meeting should be called for discussing the matter. The Committee shall discuss and decide on its jurisdiction to deal with the case or reject the complaint prima facie and recommend that no action is required to be taken in the matter.

In case credible prima facie case is made out the committee must investigate, the committee will be required to issue notice to the respondent within 7 working days of receipt of the complaint and 10 working days shall be given for submission of reply (along with the list of witnesses and documents.). The Committee will aid the aggrieved woman, if she so chooses, to file a police complaint in relation to an offence.

**If reconciliation between the two parties is a possibility**

The Committee may, before initiating an inquiry, at the request of the aggrieved woman, take steps to settle the matter between her and the respondent through conciliation.

No monetary settlement shall be made as the basis of conciliation. Where a settlement has been arrived at, the ICC shall record the settlement so arrived and forward the same to the employer for necessary compliance.

The Committee shall provide the copies of the settlement as recorded, to the aggrieved woman and the respondent. Where a settlement is arrived at, no further inquiry shall be conducted by the ICC.

**If conciliation is not feasible**

The ICC shall issue a notice to both parties for hearing. As an interim measure, ICC may recommend; the transfer of the aggrieved woman or the respondent to another section or Department as deemed fit by the Committee. grant leave to the aggrieved woman up to a period of three months or restrain the respondent from exercising any administrative authority or supervision or academic evaluation of the aggrieved woman. grant such other relief to the aggrieved woman as the case may require.

The Committee shall proceed to make inquiry into the complaint in accordance with the provisions of the service rules applicable to the respondent considering sexual harassment as misconduct.

The Presiding Officer shall convene the first hearing of the enquiry. The respondent, the aggrieved woman, and the witnesses shall be intimated at least 7 working days in advance in writing of the date, time and venue of the enquiry proceedings. The subsequent proceedings may be on a day to day basis, to be decided by ICC. The Committee shall provide reasonable opportunity to the aggrieved woman and the respondent for presenting and defending her/his case. The Committee may at any time during the enquiry proceedings, preclude the face-to- face examination of the respondent and the aggrieved woman and/or their witnesses keeping in view the need to protect the aggrieved woman or the witnesses from facing any serious health and/or safety problems. The Committee may call any person to appear as a witness if it is of the opinion that it shall be in the interest of justice. The aggrieved woman/respondent has to submit the written reply before the committee within the specified time given. The Committee shall have the right to summon, as many times as required, the respondent, aggrieved woman and/or any witnesses for the purpose of supplementary testimony and/or clarifications. The Committee shall have the power to summon any official papers or documents pertaining to the aggrieved woman as well as the respondent. The past sexual history of the aggrieved woman shall not be probed into as such information shall be deemed irrelevant to a complaint of sexual harassment.

The Committee shall have the right to terminate the enquiry proceedings and to give an ex party decision on the complaint, should the respondent fail, without valid ground, to be present for three consecutive hearings convened by the Presiding Officer.

The aggrieved woman and the respondent, or any one person on her/his behalf, shall have the right to examine written transcripts of the recordings with the exclusion of witnesses' names and identities. Any person nominated by the aggrieved woman and/or the respondent on her/his behalf shall be (only) either a student, or a member of the academic or non-teaching staff. No person who has been found guilty of sexual harassment shall be accepted as a nominee. The aggrieved woman/respondent should inform the Presiding Officer specifically if they wish to exercise this right. The Presiding Officer shall allow access to such documents on a specific date to be intimated at least two days in advance to each of the parties concerned. At no point in time, however, can the concerned parties take these documents outside the office.

The aggrieved woman and the respondent shall be responsible for presenting their witnesses before the Committee. However, if the Committee is convinced that the absence of either of the parties to the disputes is on valid grounds, the Committee shall adjourn that particular meeting of the Committee for a period not exceeding five days. The meeting so adjourned shall be conducted thereafter, even if the person concerned fails to appear for the said adjourned meeting without prior intimation/valid ground.

All proceedings of the ICC shall be recorded in writing. The record of the proceedings and the statement of witnesses shall be endorsed by the persons concerned as well as the committee members present in token of authenticity thereof. In case the minutes cannot be reduced in writing the same day, as audio recording of the proceedings may be made, and the written proceedings will be authenticated on a next available opportunity.

If the aggrieved woman desires to tender any documents by way of evidence, the Committee can supply true copies of such documents to the respondent. Similarly, if the respondent desires to tender any documents in evidence, the Committee shall supply true copies of such documents to the aggrieved woman.

In the event the Committee thinks that supplementary testimony is required, the Presiding Officer shall forward to the persons concerned a summary of the proceedings and allow for a time period of seven days to submit such testimony, in person or in writing, to the Committee. The aggrieved woman and the respondent shall have the right of cross-examination of all witnesses. However, such cross-examination shall be conducted in the form of written questions and responses via the Committee only. The respondent shall have no right to directly cross-examine the aggrieved woman or her witnesses. The respondent/aggrieved woman may submit to the Committee, a written list of questions that he/she desires to pose to the aggrieved woman/witness. The Committee (ICC) shall retain the right to disallow any questions that it has reason to believe to be irrelevant, mischievous, slanderous, derogatory or gender-insensitive. "friend of the court" (Amicus Curie) can be called for helping the committee if and when required. After conclusive investigation, the Committee shall submit a detailed reasoned report to the Institute. If the Committee finds no merit in the allegations, it shall in its wisdom conclude the investigation and submit its report. In the event the Committee finds that the allegation(s) against the respondent have been proved, it shall recommend the nature of action to be taken by the Institute. The following actions may be recommended (and / or); A written apology, Warning, Reprimand or censure, Withholding of promotion, Withholding of pay rise or increments, Undergoing a counselling session, Terminating the respondent from service, Any other punishment according to the service rules applicable to the respondent

When the Committee arrives at the conclusion that the allegation against the respondent is malicious or the aggrieved women or any other person making the complaint has made the complaint knowing it to be false or the aggrieved women or any other person making the complaint has produced any forged or misleading document, it may recommend to the Institute to take action against such falsification. Nothing precludes the ICC from taking cognizance of any new fact or evidence which may arise or be brought before it during the pendency of the inquiry proceedings or even after the communication of the findings to appropriate Institute authorities.

If the allegation(s) is/are proved against the respondent, the Committee may direct the organization to ensure the payment of compensation to the aggrieved woman by the respondent. The determination of compensation to the aggrieved woman can be decided based on; mental trauma, pain, suffering and emotional distress caused to the aggrieved woman, The loss of career opportunity due to the incident of sexual harassment, Medical expenses incurred by the victim for physical or psychiatric treatment, The income and financial status of the respondent, Feasibility of such payment in lumpsum or in instalments,

The organizations authorities will file a compliance report to the Committee within 30 days of issuance of such recommendation. ICC shall have the necessary powers to take suo motu notice of incidents of sexual harassment and/or gender injustice in the organization and act against the same in such manner as it deems appropriate. The identity of the aggrieved woman, respondent, witnesses and proceedings of the Committee and its recommendations and the action taken by the organization shall not be published, communicated or made known to the public, press or media in any manner and it will be outside the purview of the Right to Information Act, 2005.

No legal practitioner will be allowed to represent either the aggrieved woman or the respondent in proceedings before the Complaints Committee.

The Committee has the powers of a civil court in summoning and enforcing the attendance of any person related to the incident, requiring the discovery and production of any documents, any other matter relating to the incident as decided by the Committee from time to time.

## Responsibilities of the Employer and Rights of the Complainant and Respondent

**Employer**: Create and communicate a detailed policy; Ensure awareness and orientation on the issue; Constitute Complaints Committee/s in every workplace and district so that every working woman is provided with a mechanism for redress of her complaint(s); Ensure Complaints Committees are trained in both skill and capacity; Prepare an annual report and report to the respective state government.

**Rights of the Complainant**: An empathetic attitude from the Complaints Committee so that she can state her grievance in a fearless environment. A copy of the statement along with all the evidence and a list of witnesses submitted by the respondent. Keeping her identity confidential throughout the process. Support, in lodging FIR in case she chooses to lodge criminal proceedings. In case of fear of intimidation from the respondent, her statement can be recorded in absence of the respondent. Right to appeal, in case, not satisfied with the recommendations/findings of the Complaints Committee

**Rights of a Respondent**: A patient hearing to present his case in a non-biased manner; A copy of the statement along with all the evidence and a list of witnesses submitted by the complainant; Keeping his identity confidential throughout the process; Right to appeal in case not satisfied with the recommendations/findings of the Complaints

# Conclusion

Prevention is sexual harassment at the workplace is a reality and a challenge facing all our societies, regardless of which nationality we belong to. A healthy, safe and equal workplace culture is vital for the growing success of any business and professional relationship. Besides the disrepute and financial loss to the organization, it results in vitiating the work environment thus impacting business. Legislations have been and will continue to be enacted to prevent incidences of sexual harassment. Legislations can only support and reinforce, at best it can be a deterrence. Deterrence is important but cannot stand up in isolation. It is the leadership of organizations that need to stand up to the occasion. You may not be able to influence at a macro level, but you can influence what is under your influence, that is, your organization and your work culture. That will be a start and your contribution towards a safer workplace.

What better way it can be by starting to weave it into your organization's DNA.

www.ingramcontent.com/pod-product-compliance
Lightning Source LLC
Chambersburg PA
CBHW030818180526
45163CB00003B/1341